Paper Towel

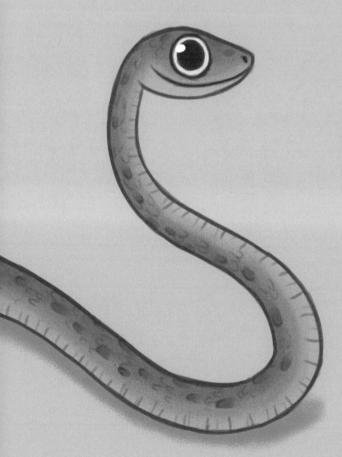

Bransen Byrd
and
Lucas Byrd

WestBow Press books may be ordered through booksellers or by contacting:

WestBow Press
A Division of Thomas Nelson & Zondervan
1663 Liberty Drive
Bloomington, IN 47403
www.westbowpress.com
1 (866) 928-1240

ISBN: 978-1-9736-6760-5 (sc)
ISBN: 978-1-9736-6761-2 (e)

Library of Congress Control Number: 2019908799

Print information available on the last page.

WestBow Press rev. date: 10/2/2019

WestBow
PRESS®
A DIVISION OF THOMAS NELSON
& ZONDERVAN

Every Sunday, Bransen and Lucas go to church with their Mom, Dad, and little brother Ryker.

One Sunday, their Sunday School teacher taught them about Jesus' love for all people, all animals, and all He had created.

The boys prayed and asked God
to show them how to love others
just like Jesus loves them.

"Oh Mom, can we keep him?" asked Lucas, "He is lost and scared." Their mom said, "Yes!" Then she asked the boys, "What will you name him?"

"We will name him...

TOWEL!"

Paper Towel loved his new home.

Soon Bransen, Lucas, and Paper Towel were playing together every day. They would play outside together.

They would eat together.

Paper Towel would ride on their tricycle with them

But one day, Paper Towe
fell off the tricycle and
hurt his eye.

Paper Towel became very sick. Bransen and Lucas prayed to God to heal him.

The next day, Bransen and Lucas' parents decided it was time for Paper Towel to live outside with other snakes like him. Because the boys loved Paper Towel, they prayed every night asking God to watch over Paper Towel and keep him safe.

Paper Towel looked everywhere for other snakes like him but did not find anyone who wanted to play with him because he looked different from them.

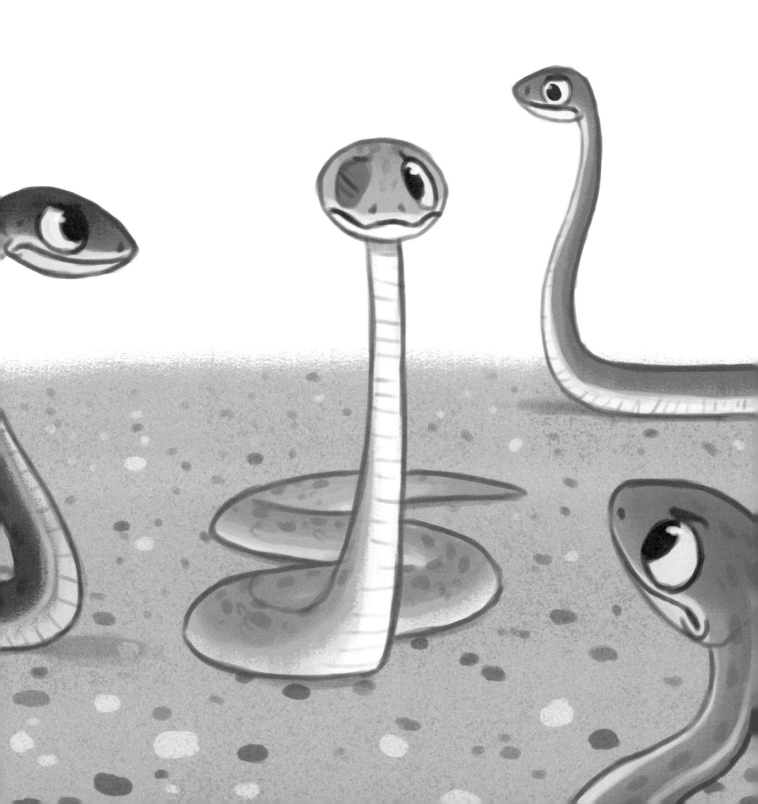

Days went by and Paper Towel missed the
boys very much.

**Paper Towel crawled back
to Bransen and Lucas'
home, lonely and sad.**

When the boys saw Paper Towel, they picked him up and gave him a great big hug.

The boys remembered that Jesus tells us to love all people, animals, and living things - especially those who are different from them. They knew that Jesus wanted them to take good care of Paper Towel.

Jesus says, "Let me give you a new commandment: 'Love one another.' This is how everyone will recognize that you are my disciples - when they see the love you have for each other and all that I have created."

Printed in the United States
By Bookmasters